Bible Study Series
for senior high

Loveland, Colorado

Why the Bible Matters
Core Belief Bible Study Series
Copyright © 1997 Group Publishing, Inc.

All rights reserved. No part of this book may be reproduced in any manner whatsoever without prior written permission from the publisher, except where noted in the text and in the case of brief quotations embodied in critical articles and reviews. For information, write Permissions, Group Publishing, Inc., Dept. PD, P.O. Box 481, Loveland, CO 80539.

Credits
Editors: Karl Leuthauser and Joani Schultz
Managing Editor: Michael D. Warden
Chief Creative Officer: Joani Schultz
Copy Editor: Julie Meiklejohn
Art Director: Lisa Chandler
Cover Art Director: Helen H. Lannis
Cover Designer/Assistant Art Director: Bill Fisher
Computer Graphic Artist: Randy Kady
Photographer: Craig DeMartino
Production Manager: Gingar Kunkel

Unless otherwise noted, Scriptures quoted from The Youth Bible, New Century Version, copyright © 1991 by Word Publishing, Dallas, Texas 75039. Used by permission.

ISBN 0-7644-0882-8

10 9 8 7 6 5 4   06 05 04 03 02 01 00 99

Printed in the United States of America.
Visit our Web site: www.grouppublishing.com

Bible Study Series
for senior high

contents:

the Core Belief: The Bible

The Word of God was written through more than forty people—on three different continents—in three different languages. Yet it communicates one theme: God's plan to reconcile sinful humanity to himself.

The Bible is God's Word to us. Through it, God establishes and deepens his relationship with us, communicating to us how he wants us to live. The Bible was written by humans—people who were inspired by the Holy Spirit to communicate God's truth accurately. Because of this, we can trust that what the Bible says is the truth.

Through the studies in this Core Christian Belief, kids can discover that they can have a closer relationship with God by reading his Word and following it. The Holy Spirit will help them accurately interpret the Bible and apply its contents to their lives.

the Helpful Stuff

THE BIBLE AS A CORE CHRISTIAN BELIEF 7
(or Why We Need a Map to Heaven)

ABOUT CORE BELIEF BIBLE STUDY SERIES 10
(or How to Move Mountains in One Hour or Less)

WHY ACTIVE AND INTERACTIVE LEARNING WORK WITH TEENAGERS 55
(or How to Keep Your Kids Awake)

YOUR EVALUATION 61
(or How You Can Edit Our Stuff Without Getting Paid)

the ▼Studies

Media Seduction 15

THE ISSUE: Youth Culture
THE BIBLE CONNECTION: Proverbs 11:2; 11:25; 14:21; 15:33; 17:9; 17:17; Matthew 10:39; 2 Timothy 3:16; and 1 John 5:12
THE POINT: The Bible can show you what's true and real about life.

Jesus Christ: Myth vs. Reality 25

THE ISSUE: Jesus
THE BIBLE CONNECTION: Matthew 8:23-32; 9:35; 28:1-10; Luke 1:26-38; 2:1-20; John 1:1-14; and 14:6-9
THE POINT: The Bible can show you the real Jesus.

Out of the Gray 35

THE ISSUE: Gray Areas of Scripture
THE BIBLE CONNECTION: 1 Corinthians 8:1-13
THE POINT: The Bible is relevant to your life.

All by Myself 45
THE ISSUE: Isolation
THE BIBLE CONNECTION: 1 Thessalonians 1:4-6 and 2 Peter 1:19-21
THE POINT: The Bible is God's Word to us.

The Bible as a Core Christian Belief

Today's young people are facing major crises concerning both who they are and who they can trust. Corruption within the ranks of religious and political leaders has propelled kids toward either a deep-seated cynicism or an apathetic disregard for most forms of authority. In addition, the emotional fallout of broken family relationships has left many kids without a clear understanding of who they are and where they belong in this chaotic world.

Fortunately, God's Word is sufficient to meet any crisis. Through the Bible, kids can learn to distinguish not only right from wrong but also "good" authority from "bad" authority. They can look in the Scriptures to discover God's true character and recognize that they're created in his image. Ultimately, they can discover God's love and realize that God desires to live in relationship with them.

In the first study of *Why the Bible Matters,* kids will take a look at **youth culture** and compare the messages the media gives to the truth the Bible offers. Students can learn that the Bible can show them what's true and real about life.

In the second study, kids will explore who **Jesus** is according to scholars and society. By looking at some of the varying perceptions of Jesus, kids can learn to look to the Bible to find the truth. They'll be encouraged by the fact that the Bible can show them the real Jesus.

The third study gives your teenagers the tools to deal with **gray areas of Scripture.** They can discover that the Bible is relevant to their lives and today's culture as they learn to apply biblical principles to issues that the Bible doesn't clearly address. Through their experiences, students can come to understand that the Bible is an excellent guide for life.

In the final study, your kids will be encouraged to look to the Bible to find God's answers. They can learn that the Bible offers help for overwhelming circumstances such as **isolation.** They'll be challenged to see that God is with them and that he communicates his truth to them through Scripture.

The Bible is God's Word to this generation of young people—just as it has been for the generations before them. The more your kids understand about the Bible, the better equipped they'll be to live as God's people in the real world.

*For a more comprehensive look at this Core Christian Belief, read Group's **Get Real: Making Core Christian Beliefs Relevant to Teenagers.***

DEPTH FINDER: WHAT CHRISTIANS BELIEVE ABOUT THE BIBLE

To help you effectively guide your kids toward this Core Christian Belief, use these overviews as a launching point for a more in-depth study of the Bible:

- **The Bible is the collection of writings recognized by the church as God's Word.** This collection of holy writings contains God's instructions for life, relationships, and service to God (Exodus 20:1-17; 31:18; Romans 3:1-2; 2 Timothy 3:15-17; and 2 Peter 1:20-21).
- **God uses the Bible to form and deepen relationships with people.** It's not enough just to learn "facts" about God. We must also seek to know God personally, based on what he has revealed about himself through his Word (Exodus 3:13-15; Isaiah 55:6-11; John 5:39-40; and Philippians 3:8-11).
- **The Bible is one of several means of communication God uses.** God also has revealed himself in creation, through prophets, through the Holy Spirit, and through his Son, Jesus Christ. Generally, today the church uses the Bible to evaluate or clarify any messages received through other means (Deuteronomy 18:15-19; Psalm 19:1-6; John 1:1-18; Acts 14:15-17; Romans 1:18-20a; and Hebrews 1:1-2).
- **The Bible is God's Word recorded by human authors.** The Holy Spirit and the human authors worked in concert with each other in such a way that God's message was communicated to us exactly as God intended (Exodus 4:12; Jeremiah 30:1-2; Romans 3:1-2; 1 Thessalonians 2:13; and 2 Peter 1:20-21).

- **The Bible tells a unified story.** From beginning to end, the Bible unfolds God's plan to reconcile sinful humanity to himself (Genesis 12:1-3; Jeremiah 31:31-34; Luke 22:14-20; 24:44-47; and John 5:46-47).
- **The Bible carries God's authority.** Because the Bible comes from God, it bears the full weight of God's authority (Deuteronomy 18:19; 28:1-2, 15, 45-46; 1 Thessalonians 2:13; and 2 Timothy 3:16a).
- **The Bible is completely trustworthy.** The Bible is an infallible guide for Christians. It's true in all that it teaches and affirms (Psalms 119:89; 160; Isaiah 40:8; and John 8:31-32; 14:26; 15:26; 16:12-13).
- **God gave us the Bible to shape our beliefs and behavior.** The Bible's teachings enable us to live peaceably with God, ourselves, and the rest of creation (Genesis 1:26–3:24; Deuteronomy 8:1-3; John 6:66-69; and 2 Timothy 3:15-17).
- **The Holy Spirit helps us apply the Bible's message to our lives.** God's Spirit shows us how the Bible should shape our beliefs and behavior in our particular situations (Psalm 119:9-18; Micah 3:8; 1 Corinthians 2:10-16; 1 Thessalonians 2:13; and Hebrews 4:12).

CORE CHRISTIAN BELIEF OVERVIEW

Here are the twenty-four Core Christian Belief categories that form the backbone of Core Belief Bible Study Series:

The Nature of God	Jesus Christ	The Holy Spirit
Humanity	Evil	Suffering
Creation	The Spiritual Realm	The Bible
Salvation	Spiritual Growth	Personal Character
God's Justice	Sin & Forgiveness	The Last Days
Love	The Church	Worship
Authority	Prayer	Family
Service	Relationships	Sharing Faith

Look for Group's Core Belief Bible Study Series books in these other Core Christian Beliefs!

about

Bible Study Series
for senior high

Think for a moment about your young people. When your students walk out of your youth program after they graduate from junior high or high school, what do you want them to know? What foundation do you want them to have so they can make wise choices?

You probably want them to know the essentials of the Christian faith. You want them to base everything they do on the foundational truths of Christianity. Are you meeting this goal?

If you have any doubt that your kids will walk into adulthood knowing and living by the tenets of the Christian faith, then you've picked up the right book. All the books in Group's Core Belief Bible Study Series encourage young people to discover the essentials of Christianity and to put those essentials into practice. Let us explain...

What Is Group's Core Belief Bible Study Series?

Group's Core Belief Bible Study Series is a biblically in-depth study series for junior high and senior high teenagers. This Bible study series utilizes four defining commitments to create each study. These "plumb lines" provide structure and continuity for every activity, study, project, and discussion. They are:

- **A Commitment to Biblical Depth**—Core Belief Bible Study Series is founded on the belief that kids not only *can* understand the deeper truths of the Bible but also *want* to understand them. Therefore, the activities and studies in this series strive to explain the "why" behind every truth we explore. That way, kids learn principles, not just rules.

- **A Commitment to Relevance**—Most kids aren't interested in abstract theories or doctrines about the universe. They want to know how to live successfully right now, today, in the heat of problems they can't ignore. Because of this, each study connects a real-life need with biblical principles that speak directly to that need. This study series finally bridges the gap between Bible truths and the real-world issues kids face.

- **A Commitment to Variety**—Today's young people have been raised in a sound bite world. They demand variety. For that reason, no two meetings in this study series are shaped exactly the same.

- **A Commitment to Active and Interactive Learning**—Active learning is learning by doing. Interactive learning simply takes active learning a step further by having kids teach each other what they've learned. It's a process that helps kids internalize and remember their discoveries.

For a more detailed description of these concepts, see the section titled "Why Active and Interactive Learning Works With Teenagers" beginning on page 55.

So how can you accomplish all this in a set of four easy-to-lead Bible studies? By weaving together various "power" elements to produce a fun experience that leaves kids challenged and encouraged.

Turn the page to take a look at some of the power elements used in this series.

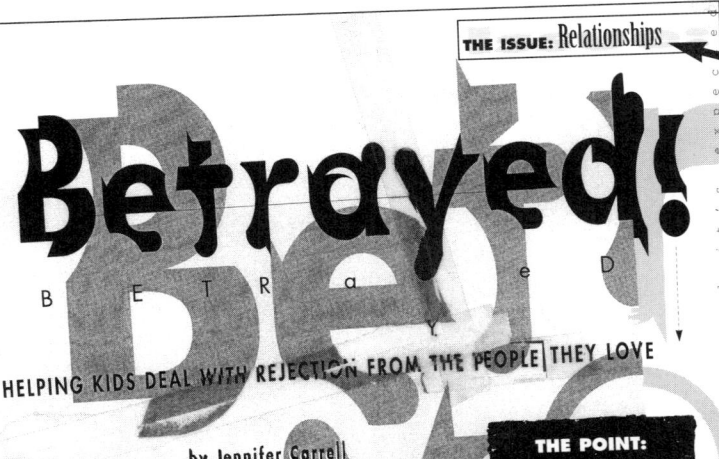

- **A Relevant Topic**—More than ever before, kids live in the now. What matters to them and what attracts their hearts is what's happening in their world at this moment. For this reason, every Core Belief Bible Study focuses on a particular hot topic that kids care about.

- **A Core Christian Belief**—Group's Core Belief Bible Study Series organizes the wealth of Christian truth and experience into twenty-four Core Christian Belief categories. These twenty-four headings act as umbrellas for a collection of detailed beliefs that define Christianity and set it apart from the world and every other religion. Each book in this series features one Core Christian Belief with lessons suited for junior high or senior high students.

  "But," you ask, "won't my kids be bored talking about all these spiritual beliefs?" No way! As a youth leader, you know the value of using hot topics to connect with young people. Ultimately teenagers talk about issues because they're searching for meaning in their lives. They want to find the one equation that will make sense of all the confusing events happening around them. Each Core Belief Bible Study answers that need by connecting a hot topic with a powerful Christian principle. Kids walk away from the study with something more solid than just the shifting ebb and flow of their own opinions. They walk away with a deeper understanding of their Christian faith.

- **The Point**—This simple statement is designed to be the intersection between the Core Christian Belief and the hot topic. Everything in the study ultimately focuses on The Point so that kids study it and allow it time to sink into their hearts.

- **The Study at a Glance**—A quick look at this chart will tell you what kids will do, how long it will take them to do it, and what supplies you'll need to get it done.

Helpful Stuff 11

- **The Bible Connection**—This is the power base of each study. Whether it's just one verse or several chapters, The Bible Connection provides the vital link between kids' minds and their hearts. The content of each Core Belief Bible Study reflects the belief that the true power of God—the power to expose, heal, and change kids' lives—is contained in his Word.

THE POINT OF *BETRAYED!*:

God is love.

THE BIBLE CONNECTION

1 JOHN 4:7-21 — The Apostle John explains the nature and definition of perfect love.

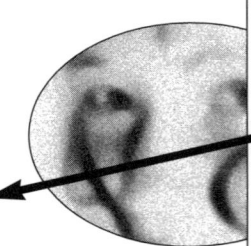

In this study, kids will compare the imperfect love defined in real-life stories of betrayal to God's definition of perfect love.

By making this comparison, kids can discover that God is love and therefore incapable of betraying them. Then they'll be able to recognize the incredible opportunity God offers to experience the only relationship worthy of their absolute trust.

Explore the verses in The Bible Connect mation in the Depthfinder boxes throughou understanding of how these Scriptures con

LEADER TIP for The Study

THE STUDY

DISCUSSION STARTER ▼

Jump-Start (up to 5 minutes) As kids arrive, ask them to thi common themes in movies, books, TV sho have kids each contribute ideas for a mas two other kids in the room and sharing sider providing copies of People maga what's currently showing on television or at their suggestions, write their respo come up with a lot of great ide ent, look through this list an try to disc ments most of these theme have in com

After kids make several s gestions, ment responses are connected with the idea of bet

● **Why do you think betrayal is such a**

Betrayed! 17

LEADER TIP for The Study

Because this topic can be so powerful and relevant to kids' lives, your group members may be tempted to get caught up in issues and lose sight of the deeper biblical principle found in The Point. Help your kids grasp The Point by guiding kids to focus on the biblical investigation and discussing how God's truth connects with reality in their lives.

DEPTHFINDER UNDERSTANDING INTEGRITY

Your students may not be entirely familiar with the meaning of integrity, especially as it might apply to God's character in the Trinity. Use these definitions (taken from Webster's II New Riverside Dictionary) and other information to help you guide kids toward a better understanding of how God maintains integrity through the three expressions of the Trinity.

Integrity: 1. Firm adherence to a code or standard of values. 2. The state of being unimpaired. 3. The quality or condition of being undivided.

Synonyms for integrity include probity, completeness, wholeness, soundness, and perfection.

Our word "integrity" comes from the Latin word *integritas*, which means soundness. *Integritas* is also the root of the word "integer," which means "whole or complete," as in a "whole" number.

The Hebrew word that's often translated "integrity" (for example, in Psalm 25:21 [NIV]) is *tam*. It means whole, perfect, sincere, and honest.

CREATIVE GOD-EXPLORATION ▼

Top Hats (18 to 20 minutes) Form three groups, with each trio member from the previous activity going to a different group. Give each group Bibles, paper, and pens, and assign each group a different hat God wears: Father, Son, or Holy Spirit.

- **Depthfinder Boxes**— These informative sidelights located throughout each study add insight into a particular passage, word, historical fact, or Christian doctrine. Depthfinder boxes also provide insight into teen culture, adolescent development, current events, and philosophy.

Holy Profiles

Your assigned Bible passage describes how a particular person or group responded when confronted with God's holiness. Use the information in your passage to help your group discuss the questions below. Then use your flashlights to teach the other two groups what you discover.

■ Based on your passage, what does holiness look like?

■ What does holiness sound like?

■ When people see God's holiness, how does it affect them?

■ How is this response to God's holiness like humility?

■ Based on your passage, how would you describe humility?

■ Why is humility an appropriate human response to God's holiness?

■ Based on what you see in your passage, do you think you are a humble person? Why or why not?

■ What's one way you could develop humility in your life this week?

Permission to photocopy this handout from Group's Core Belief Bible Study Series granted for local church use. Copyright © Group Publishing, Inc., Box 481, Loveland, CO 80539.

- **Leader Tips**— These handy information boxes coach you through the study, offering helpful suggestions on everything from altering activities for different-sized groups to streamlining discussions to using effective discipline techniques.

- **Handouts**—Most Core Belief Bible Studies include photocopiable handouts to use with your group. Handouts might take the form of a fun game, a lively discussion starter, or a challenging study page for kids to take home—anything to make your study more meaningful and effective.

Helpful Stuff 12

The Last Word on Core Belief Bible Studies

Soon after you begin to use Group's Core Belief Bible Study Series, you'll see signs of real growth in your group members. Your kids will gain a deeper understanding of the Bible and of their own Christian faith. They'll see more clearly how a relationship with Jesus affects their daily lives. And they'll grow closer to God.

But that's not all. You'll also see kids grow closer to one another.

That's because this series is founded on the principle that Christian faith grows best in the context of relationship. Each study uses a variety of interactive pairs and small groups and always includes discussion questions that promote deeper relationships. The friendships kids will build through this study series will enable them to grow *together* toward a deeper relationship with God.

THE ISSUE: Youth Culture

Media Seduction

The High-Tech Battle for the Heart of a Generation

by Michael D. Warden

THE POINT: The Bible can show you what's true and real about life.

■ Entertainment does far more than just entertain. Through movies, TV shows, music videos, and commercials, today's entertainment industry has become one of the most powerful influencers of young people—in everything from clothing styles, to sports heroes, to music, to beliefs about the nature and value of life itself. ■ Like electronic elder siblings, television and movies guide kids through their teenage years, telling them what to believe and what to avoid, who to trust and who to ignore. Not all the messages get through, of course. But the teenagers are listening. ■ This study examines the effects of the media on kids' views about life and reality and exposes pop-culture lies under the true light of the only reliable source of truth—God's Word.

The Study AT A GLANCE

SECTION	MINUTES	WHAT STUDENTS WILL DO	SUPPLIES
Relational Time	up to 5	ONE TRUE THING—Tell about one belief they have about life.	
Comparative Study	15 to 20	DESIGNER REALITIES—Create live characters based on pop culture and biblical character traits.	Bibles, paper, pencils, pop-culture and music magazines, TV Guide magazine, index cards, tape
Interactive Narration	15 to 20	REALITY MASTERS—Guide their characters through real-life experiences to see how they'll respond.	Index cards, pencils, tape
Pair Discussions	5 to 10	BACK IN THE REAL WORLD—Compare their own view of reality with the two characters' views.	Bible
Prayer Experience	5 to 10	A CULTURE OF TRUTH—Create personal character goals based on what they've learned.	Index cards, pencils

notes:

THE POINT OF **MEDIA SEDUCTION:**

The Bible can show you what's true and real about life.

THE BIBLE CONNECTION

PROVERBS 11:2; 11:25; 14:21; 15:33; 17:9; 17:17; MATTHEW 10:39; 1 JOHN 5:12	These verses pinpoint several character traits essential to godliness.
2 TIMOTHY 3:16	Paul instructs Timothy about using Scripture as a guide to Christlike character and truth.

In this study, kids will work together to create two "live" characters—one patterned after pop culture, the other patterned after Bible truth—then send them into several real-life scenarios to see how they respond.

By comparing these two characters' choices, kids can discover how pop culture tries to delude them and how the Bible provides the most reliable instruction for dealing with real-life issues.

Explore the verses in the Bible Connection box, then read the information in the Depthfinder boxes throughout the study to gain a deeper understanding of how these Scriptures connect with your young people.

LEADER TIP for The Study

To improve the flow of the study, write a list of the Scriptures in the Bible Connection box on a piece of paper before you begin.

THE STUDY

RELATIONAL TIME ▼

One True Thing (up to 5 minutes) Have kids form trios. In their trios, ask kids each to tell one belief they have about life. For example, someone might say, "I believe the bad you do comes back to you" or "I believe in myself." After everyone has shared, have a person from each trio report back to the whole group all the beliefs kids talked about.

Next, have kids each tell their trios where their belief came from; for

LEADER TIP for The Study

Whenever groups discuss a list of questions, write the questions on newsprint and tape the newsprint to the wall so groups can answer the questions at their own pace.

Media Seduction 17

LEADER TIP for Designer Realities

If you have access to a television and VCR, consider recording snippets of music videos and TV shows popular with teenagers. You could also show short clips from popular movies that you think promote a particular belief about life. Let the "pop culture" group members use the clips to help them choose their seven pop-culture traits.

LEADER TIP for Designer Realities

To help kids define or understand the biblical meanings for terms such as humble, contrite, or prideful, provide them with a regular dictionary as well as a biblical dictionary. Encourage kids to look up any words that sound confusing to them.

example, "My mother told me" or "I heard it in a song." After everyone has shared, have a new person from each trio tell the whole group what that trio discussed. Then ask:

● **Why do you suppose we get our beliefs about life from different sources?**

● **Does it matter which sources you depend on to tell you how you should live? Why or why not?**

● **How much does the media influence what you believe is true about life? Explain.**

Say: **Today we'll explore the beliefs promoted by the media and pop culture and see how they stand up when compared to the truth about life described in the Bible. The media and pop culture may try to sell you on their version of reality, but only <u>the Bible can show you what's true and real about life.</u>**

COMPARATIVE STUDY ▼

Designer Realities (15 to 20 minutes) Form two groups, and give each group index cards and pencils. Give one group a stack of pop-culture and music magazines, along with a TV Guide magazine for that week. Instruct that group to study the advertisements, articles, and TV shows listed in their publications and come up with seven personality qualities that define what being "wise" in pop culture is all about. For example, kids might list qualities such as these: "You always protect the earth" or "You value your own self-fulfillment over all else." Challenge kids to make the qualities as specific and accurate as possible.

Give the other group a set of Bibles and a list of the passages from the Bible Connection box. Have that group explore each of the passages listed and come up with seven personality qualities that define what being "wise" in life is all about from God's point of view. For example, kids might list qualities such as these: "You're humble" or "You're willing to forgive people who hurt you."

DEPTHFINDER — UNDERSTANDING THESE KIDS

Your young people may want to deny that media have any influence at all on their attitudes and behaviors, but deep down they know that television, movies, and music are having an effect on them.

In a survey conducted by the George H. Gallup International Institute, kids today ranked music and television as two of the top six factors they believe have the greatest influence on their generation. So, despite their arguments to the contrary, kids know that the media is impacting them, even if they don't realize how much or in what ways its effect is felt.

Here's how music and television fit in with other influencers kids said were the most powerful: (1) friends, (2) home, (3) school, (4) music, (5) television, and (6) religion.

Media Seduction   18

When groups have decided on their seven traits, have them write each trait on a separate index card. Then ask a volunteer from each group to explain to the rest of the class the seven traits his or her group chose. Ask:

● **Who here has ever played a computer role-playing game where you create a character and then guide it through several adventures?**

Ask some of those who raise their hands to describe how those computer games work. Then say: **Today we're going to experience a similar kind of role-playing game. We're going to reprogram two people in this room to become characters in our own role-playing adventure.**

Have each group choose one person to reprogram as an interactive game character.

Say: **You can reprogram your character by assigning him or her the seven personality qualities your group came up with earlier. These traits will dictate how your character will respond in all the situations we create.**

Have groups tape the seven traits onto the characters as a sign of "reprogramming." Then have each group create a name for its character, write it on an index card, and tape it to his or her chin.

Stand the two characters in the front of the room. Review the personality qualities that define each character, then say: **Now we're just about ready to take our two characters on a little adventure through the real world.**

LEADER TIP for Reality Masters

If someone in your class is gifted in dramatic presentation, consider asking him or her to read the scenarios instead of you. If you do this, however, be sure the reader knows to stop at the "Freeze frame!" command, and that he or she allows the actors time to act out what's being read.

INTERACTIVE NARRATION ▼

Reality Masters (15 to 20 minutes) Clear a large space in the room for all the action to take place. Tell both groups that you're going to read a series of "Reality Master" scenarios and that both groups' characters will act out the scene together. Then say: **Every so often, I'll call out, "Freeze frame!" to stop the action so your group can make a decision about what your character will do next. Before we start the action, we need a few other characters to act out some additional parts of the story.**

Ask for volunteers to play the following parts: Shannon, Mom, and Stepdad. Write each character's name on an index card, and tape it to the appropriate person's chin. Tell the characters to stay in their groups until they are cued and then just come to the open space and follow the narration's instructions.

Once all the characters are chosen and ready, start reading this scenario: **You're in your school hallway, carrying your books. You like coming to school, but not because of the classes. You like school because you have several classes with "that special person" in your life. With each step you take toward your next class, you feel more and more like you're falling in love. You think this could be the person you want to spend your life with.**

Around the corner, you find one of your school friends, Shannon.

Media Seduction   19

LEADER TIP for Reality Masters

The scenarios kids will deal with in this activity may be similar to situations some of them face in real life. Encourage kids to be sensitive to each issue you discuss by avoiding hurtful jokes and comments. Also, encourage kids who may be dealing with any of these issues to come pray with you privately after the study.

Shannon pulls you over to the corner of the room. "I'm sorry to be the one to have to tell you this," says Shannon, "but I thought it'd be best to hear it from a friend."

You shake Shannon. "What is it?"

Shannon sighs. "Well, it's like this. Last night the whole cheerleading squad went to the drive-in together. While they were there, they spied your truelove making out with your best friend. They were in his red Mustang. Anyway, today it's the talk of the school. I'm sorry to have to tell you, but I thought you had a right to know." Freeze frame!

In their groups, have kids answer this question:
● **Based on the personality traits you selected, how would your character most likely deal with this situation?**

After one minute, have a volunteer from each group explain how they think their character would respond. Then ask:
● **Which character's response do you think is best? Explain.**
● **If your character did as you suggest, what do you think would be the long-term results or consequences of his or her actions? Explain.**

After a few minutes of discussion, continue the action: **The rest of your day was awful. You worked for six hours at Pablo's House of Tacos, and now you're finally home—exhausted. Quietly, you step through the front door and tiptoe through the living room so you don't wake your mom and stepdad.**

Suddenly, you hear a scream upstairs.

Quickly, you run upstairs. You hear another cry. This time you're sure it's your mom, and the sounds are coming from her bedroom. Believing that surprise is your ally, you bust through the door.

In the bedroom, you see your mother sitting on the bed in her robe. Her face is red, and she's crying. You see your stepfather standing over her. His face is angry. When he looks up and sees you, he shouts, "Get out!" Freeze frame!

In their groups, have kids answer this question:
● **Based on the personality traits you selected, how would your character most likely deal with this situation?**

After one minute, have volunteers from each group explain how his or her character would respond. Then ask:
● **Which character's response do you think is best? Explain.**
● **If your character did as you suggest, what do you think would be the long-term results or consequences of his or her actions? Explain.**

After a few minutes of discussion, continue the action with the third scenario: **Your friend from church calls you the next day. He wants you to go out with the youth group to take in a movie. You almost say yes, but then he tells you that Jamie will be there, and you hesitate.**

You and Jamie have gotten to be close friends lately. You've been doing just about everything together. There really shouldn't be a problem, but lately your feelings have changed. They're getting stronger, deeper, and you're not sure what to do about it. You

Media Seduction   20

don't think Jamie suspects. You don't think anybody suspects. But you're definitely feeling it, and it's all too confusing for you to handle.

If it was like any other relationship, it would be easier to deal with. But it's not, because you and Jamie are both the same gender. Freeze frame!

In their groups, have kids answer this question:
● **Based on the personality traits you selected, how would your character most likely deal with this situation?**

After one minute, have volunteers from each group explain how they think their characters would respond. Then ask:
● **Which character's response do you think is best? Explain.**
● **If your character did as you suggest, what do you think would be the long-term results or consequences of his or her actions? Explain.**

LEADER TIP for The Study

Because this topic can be so powerful and relevant to kids' lives, your group members may be tempted to get caught up in issues and lose sight of the deeper biblical principle found in The Point. Help your kids grasp The Point by guiding them to focus on the biblical investigation and discussing how God's truth connects with reality in their lives.

PAIR DISCUSSIONS ▼

Back in the Real World (5 to 10 minutes)

Congratulate the groups on their successful interactive experience, then say: **Now let's make our interaction a little more personal.**

Have kids each find a partner, then have partners discuss the following questions. After every question, have a few pairs report back to the whole group what they discussed. Ask:
● **What did you discover about the difference between the Christ-like character's actions and the pop-culture character's actions?**
● **What does this experience tell you about the reliability of pop culture and the media to teach you about real life?**
● **What does this experience tell you about the reliability of the Bible to teach you about real life?**
● **What's the best way to learn the "wisdom for living" contained in the Bible?**

DEPTHFINDER UNDERSTANDING THESE KIDS

Your kids may initially balk at the idea that the Bible is the only source of wisdom they can trust. Don't let that reaction surprise you. Today's kids are growing up in a world that no longer believes in absolutes. According to the Barna Research Group, 70 percent of kids "claim that absolute truth does not exist" and "that all truth is relative and personal."

Believing there are no absolutes creates a great problem for kids, because it leaves them with nothing and no one they can trust with absolute certainty. Thankfully, God's Word offers an answer to this dilemma. Not only does the Bible provide the only real absolutes kids need to believe in, it also opens the door to the most trustworthy relationship they can ever experience.

DEPTHFINDER: UNDERSTANDING THE BIBLE

Before discussing the Reality Masters scenarios with your group, you may want to delve into Scripture more deeply to see what the Bible has to say to kids who might be struggling in these areas. Here are some suggested passages to get you started.

For Scenario 1: Judges 16; Matthew 6:9-15; 18:15-17; Romans 13:8-14; and Ephesians 4:25-32.

For Scenario 2: Psalm 11:4-7; Proverbs 4:14-17; 29:11; Ephesians 5:25; and James 1:19-21.

For Scenario 3: Romans 8:1-16, 35-39; 1 Corinthians 6:9-11; 10:13; 2 Corinthians 10:3-5; and 1 Thessalonians 4:3-8.

Read aloud 2 Timothy 3:16, then say: **Pop culture and the media aren't the only voices fighting for your attention these days. And every voice you hear is trying to tell you how it thinks you should live. Examining what these voices have to say is fine, as long as you remember that only <u>the Bible can show you what's true and real about life.</u>**

All Scripture is given by **GOD** and is **useful for teaching,** FOR **showing people what is wrong in their lives,** for correcting faults, AND *for teaching how to live* right.

2 TIMOTHY 3:16

Media Seduction

PRAYER EXPERIENCE ▼

A Culture of Truth

(5 to 10 minutes)

Give each person an index card and a pencil. Say: **Now that you've had practice creating an imaginary character, you can use the same process on yourself—only this time it's real. On your card, write one character quality you want in your life. Consider all that we've learned today, and remember the Christlike character traits we came up with as you think about the quality you want.**

Once kids have finished, have them form a huddle. (If you have more than twelve kids, form two huddles.) Tell kids you're going to guide them through a prayer experience in which they'll get to pray for one another. One at a time, have kids stand in the center of the circle and tell the group what they wrote on their cards. As each person stands in the center, ask the other group members each to place one hand on the center person's shoulders.

Encourage kids to pray aloud, at their own discretion, for God to build into the center person the quality he or she chose. Also encourage kids to thank God aloud for specific positive character qualities that person already has.

After each person has been prayed for by two or three people, place a new person in the center of the huddle, and have kids pray again. Continue until everyone has been prayed for and encouraged.

Close the experience by asking God to help kids learn to rely on the <u>Bible as their only trustworthy source of wisdom for living in the real world.</u>

THE ISSUE: Jesus

Jesus Christ: Myth vs. Reality

BY PAUL WOODS

THE POINT:

The Bible can show you the real Jesus.

■ "Who, Jesus? Isn't he that righteous dead dude?" That's just one young man's response to the question, "Who is Jesus?" There are more. A lot more, from great minds all over the world: "Jesus was a good man" " ...a great teacher" " ...an advanced soul" " ...a prophet" " ...a feminist" " ...a fictional character" " ...a political revolutionary" " ...a failure." ■ Everyone seems ready to spout opinions, but the truth about Christ's personality and purpose still remains a mystery to most of the world. ■ And, possibly, to your kids. ■ In this study, your young people will examine opinions about Jesus from leaders of several world religions. And they'll discover that, despite the myriad of public opinions, there's one reliable place they can go to discover the real Jesus—the Bible.

The Study
AT A GLANCE

SECTION	MINUTES	WHAT STUDENTS WILL DO	SUPPLIES
Relational Time	up to 5	GETTING TO KNOW YOU—Talk about how others can get to know them.	
Investigation 1	15 to 20	CREATE-YOUR-OWN JESUS—Form groups, and put together an image of what they hope Jesus looks like.	Newsprint, markers, tape
Investigation 2	25 to 30	WHO DO THEY SAY HE IS?—Examine magazines, scholars' quotes, and Bible passages to seek who Jesus really is.	Bibles; newsprint; markers; copies of Newsweek, People, and Rolling Stone magazines; "The Scholars Say..." handout (p. 33); "The Real Jesus" Depthfinder (p. 31)
Reflections	5 to 10	ART CRITIQUES—Discuss their discoveries about Jesus from the various sources, and determine which one is most accurate.	Bibles, newsprint, images of Jesus

notes:

THE POINT OF *JESUS CHRIST: MYTH VS. REALITY:*

The Bible can show you the real Jesus.

THE BIBLE CONNECTION

MATTHEW 8:23-32; 9:35; 28:1-10; LUKE 1:26-38; 2:1-20; JOHN 1:1-14; 14:6-9

These passages give key insights into who Jesus is—starting at the Creation and proceeding through his birth, his teachings and actions, then continuing through his death and resurrection.

In this study, kids will create their own representations of Jesus and examine depictions of Jesus from magazines, from scholarly circles, and from the Bible.

By examining these various views of Jesus, kids can begin to see that our culture's image of Jesus is only an illusion and that the Bible shows us the real Jesus.

Explore the verses in The Bible Connection, then examine the information in the Depthfinder boxes throughout the study to gain a deeper understanding of how these Scriptures connect with your young people.

LEADER TIP for The Study

Whenever groups discuss a list of questions, write the questions on newsprint and tape the newsprint to the wall so groups can answer the questions at their own pace.

BEFORE THE STUDY

Write these questions on newsprint, and tape the newsprint to the wall:
- How can someone really get to know you?
- Who really knows you well?
- Do you believe that Jesus really knows you? Why or why not?
- How well do you know Jesus? Explain.

Make one copy of "The Real Jesus" Depthfinder (p. 31).

Jesus Christ: Myth vs. Reality   27

THE STUDY

RELATIONAL TIME ▼

Getting to Know You (up to 5 minutes)
As kids arrive, have them each find a partner to discuss the first question on the sheet of newsprint that you taped to the wall. After one minute, have kids find new partners to discuss the second question. Continue until all the questions have been discussed.

INVESTIGATION 1 ▼

Create-Your-Own Jesus (15 to 20 minutes)
Form three groups. Give each group a set of colored markers and a "supersize" sheet of newsprint. Have groups each trace the outline of one group member onto the newsprint. Say: **Now we're going to do a little creating. Think about this question:**
- **If you could create your own "custom" Jesus—who would be with you throughout your life—what would he be like?**

In your group, work together to create a custom portrait of Jesus in detail. Draw features on the body, write character traits inside the outline, or draw symbols or pictures of how this Jesus would act. Limit yourselves to seven or fewer ideas. When all the drawings are ready, we'll tape them to the wall and create a "Jesus Portrait Gallery."

> **LEADER TIP for Create-Your-Own Jesus**
>
> If you have more than thirty kids, form six groups instead of three. That will make the study flow more smoothly when these same groups work together during the "Who Do They Say He Is?" activity.

> **DEPTH FINDER — UNDERSTANDING THESE TEENAGERS**
>
> One form of media that affects teenagers even more powerfully than magazines or music is television. Unfortunately, television doesn't often present a positive or accurate image of Jesus. In his groundbreaking study titled *Watching America*, Professor Stanley Rothman has shown that instead of reflecting a realistic picture of American beliefs, television typically reflects the biases and views of those who create the programming. Which, in turn, means your kids may get a skewed message about who Jesus really is.
>
> For example, 93 percent of television's creative leaders say they never or seldom attend religious services. Over 50 percent of that same group claim that God plays no role in society today. In fact, many of the television industry leaders say that the influence of religion and God on society has been "detrimental."
>
> The impact of these views on your kids' lives is subtle yet undeniable. Television influences teenagers. And, when it comes to describing the real Jesus, television lies.

Jesus Christ: Myth vs. Reality   28

DEPTHFINDER
UNDERSTANDING THE BIBLE

In John 10:11-15 Jesus speaks of himself as the Good Shepherd and his people as sheep. Jesus often used this sheep imagery when referring to people. And it's not hard to see why. Sheep are known to be followers. In fact, they've even been known to blindly follow each other right off of a cliff. Animals like that need lots of care and guidance—just like us.

When groups are ready, have them tape their portraits of Jesus on the wall and explain them. Ask:
• **How did you feel working with your group to create your own custom Jesus?**
• **Did you agree with all of your group members' suggestions for what Jesus should be like? Why or why not?**
• **How are our perceptions of Jesus alike? different?**
• **How is creating our own Jesus like what a lot of people do with Jesus in real life?**

Say: **Today we're going to be taking a close look at several people's opinions of who Jesus is. Through our investigation, we'll discover that** the Bible can show us the real Jesus. **Right now, find a partner and pray together, asking God to guide us as we examine what different people say about Jesus.**

LEADER TIP for Who Do They Say He Is?

While groups are working, copy the assigned Bible passages onto newsprint so everyone can see them. The whole group will use them later in the study.

INVESTIGATION 2 ▼

Who Do They Say He Is? (25 to 30 minutes)

Have kids stay in their groups. Give each group another supersize sheet of newsprint, and have groups each trace a different group member's outline on the paper. Then give each group one of the following sets of materials:

Set 1: One copy each of Newsweek, Rolling Stone, and People magazines
Set 2: A copy of "The Scholars Say..." handout (p. 33)
Set 3: A copy of "The Real Jesus" Depthfinder (p. 31)

Say: **Using only the information you've been given, create a new picture of Jesus that illustrates what your information teaches. For example, if your information describes Jesus as a radical feminist, you could draw him with a pro-woman picket sign in his hand. Give your Jesus portrait a title based on the source of your information. When you're finished, we'll add your new Jesus to our Jesus Portrait Gallery.**

After fifteen to twenty minutes, have groups present their findings. Remind groups not to criticize each other's presentations or artwork. Say: **There are lots of different images of Jesus portrayed in our world. But only** the Bible can tell us who the real Jesus is.

LEADER TIP for Who Do They Say He Is?

Since the magazines given to one group will probably not say much about who Jesus is, encourage kids to formulate what they think the magazines might say about Jesus. For an idea of what that might be, have kids look at what the magazines present as appropriate beliefs, lifestyles, behavior, role models, and the like.

Jesus Christ: Myth vs. Reality   29

LEADER TIP for The Study

Because this topic can be so powerful and relevant to kids' lives, your group members may be tempted to get caught up in issues and lose sight of the deeper biblical principle found in The Point. Help your kids grasp The Point by guiding them to focus on the biblical investigation and discussing how God's truth connects with reality in their lives.

Jesus *answered,*
"I am the way,
and the truth,
and the life.
The ONLY way to the **FATHER** is through **me.**
If you REALLY KNEW ME, you would know
my **FATHER**, *too.*
But now you *do know him,*
and you have *seen him.*"
Philip said to him,
*"Lord, show us the Father.
That is all we need."*
Jesus *answered,*
"I have been with you a long time now.
Do you still NOT KNOW ME, Philip?
Whoever has seen **me** has seen the **FATHER.**
So why do you say,
'Show us the FATHER'?"

JOHN 14:6-9

DEPTHFINDER — UNDERSTANDING THESE TEENAGERS

When it comes to God, his Son Jesus, and Christianity, just what do the majority of teenagers believe to be the truth? In his research-based book, *Baby Busters: Disillusioned Generation*, George Barna lists some of the firmly held religious beliefs of today's generation. Here's a sampling:

BELIEF STATEMENT	PERCENTAGE OF PEOPLE WHO STRONGLY AGREE
There is only one God; he created the universe and rules it today.	66%
Jesus Christ, who is God's Son, rose from the dead and is alive today.	50%
The Bible is the Word of God and is totally accurate in all that it teaches.	44%
Christians, Jews, Buddhists, Muslims, and all others pray to the same god, even though they use different names for that god.	33%
All good people will go to heaven when they die.	27%
The Christian faith has all the answers to leading a successful life.	23%

Jesus Christ: Myth vs. Reality   30

REFLECTIONS ▼

Art Critiques (5 to 10 minutes) Display each group's new depiction of Jesus on the wall so everyone can see it. Have kids form trios consisting of one person from each of the previous study groups. Have each group choose an Asker to keep everyone focused on the questions, a Recorder to keep track of the discussion, and a Reporter to share the group's conclusions with the rest of the class. Say: **Now you're going to be art critics. In your groups, discuss what's real and what's an illusion about each of these depictions of Jesus on the wall. Look at some of the passages of Scripture given earlier to help you. Use these questions to guide your discussion as you look at each drawing:**

- **How is the depiction like or unlike the real Jesus?**
- **How is the depiction like an advertisement—an illusion someone is trying to sell to our society?**
- **How could the Bible help someone decide whether this depiction represents the real Jesus?**

DEPTHFINDER — THE REAL JESUS

Let these passages help you gain a clearer picture of the real Jesus according to the Bible:

John 1:1-14—Jesus has existed forever. He was with God and was active in Creation. The term "Word," referring to Jesus, carries a much deeper meaning than the "Word of God" as we think of it. In the original Greek, the word means unique thoughts that powerfully convey the mind of the author. Thus, in Jesus, God has shown us himself.

Luke 1:26-38 and 2:1-20—Jesus' birth was announced to Mary through an angel who made it clear that Jesus would be supernaturally conceived—without doubt the Son of God. And when Jesus was born, God sent angels to deliver the birth announcement to earth. Shepherds—considered some of the lowliest people on earth—were the first to hear that the Savior had been born.

Matthew 8:23-32—Jesus demonstrated power over both the natural world and the spiritual world by calming the storm and driving out demons. It's interesting to note that Jesus' disciples wondered who he really was, but the demons recognized him immediately as the Son of God.

Matthew 9:35—Jesus wasn't just bent on demonstrating his mighty power; he was a man of compassion. Though his teachings were important, he always had enough time—and love—to take care of hurting people.

John 14:6-9—Jesus made it clear that he is the only way through which we can have a relationship with the Father. In fact, he actually claims divinity, insisting that the Father is in him and that he is in the Father.

Matthew 28:1-10—Jesus' death on the cross wasn't an unexpected tragedy but part of a glorious plan to defeat death. Notice that the first to hear of Jesus' resurrection and to see him were women—second-class citizens in the culture of that day.

Permission to photocopy this Depthfinder from Group's Core Belief Bible Study Series granted for local church use. Copyright © Group Publishing, Inc., P.O. Box 481, Loveland, CO 80539.

Jesus Christ: Myth vs. Reality

After about one or two minutes of discussion about each newsprint picture, have groups move on to the next one. When groups have examined all the pictures, have the reporters share what they discussed with the rest of the class.

Say: **There are lots of images of Jesus that people would like us to believe, but <u>the Bible shows us the real Jesus.</u>**

Ask:

● **Has your picture of Jesus changed since the beginning of the study? Why or why not?**

● **How have the opinions of other people or of our culture affected the way you see Jesus? Explain.**

● **How can you counter the impact that other people's ideas about Jesus has on your life? on your friends' lives?**

● **Why is the Bible so important to help you understand the real Jesus?**

Have kids find partners to discuss these final questions:

● **How would understanding and believing in the real Jesus change the way you live?**

● **What's one thing you'll do this week to understand the real Jesus better?**

Have pairs close by praying together, asking God to help them grow in their understanding and commitment to the real Jesus.

THE Scholars Say...

"Greek Orthodox theologians say the main purpose of Jesus was to bring God and man closer, but not necessarily to die in that atoning way we've developed in the West. Their favorite image of Jesus is not the crucified figure but the transfigured, when the divinity shines through him, rather like the image of Buddha sitting under the bo tree—the example of a deified humanity, which we shall all be like one day."

—Karen Armstrong, Professor of Religion at Leo Baeck College, author of *A History of God*

"Jesus, to succeed, *had* to choose martyrdom. He had been a failure in all sorts of human enterprises. One was to convert everybody to love, to turning the other cheek. He was an abysmal failure at that. He was also a failure in his more militant role—scourging the moneylenders, and so forth. He changed nothing. So, basically, the only power he had at the end was the power of abdication."

—Peter A. Bien, professor of English at Dartmouth College, translator of *The Last Temptation of Christ*

"He was a feminist. He cured ill women, allowed them to become people who related his truths, forgave a repentant prostitute, allowed her to touch him. Women gave their money to support him. Mary Magdalen was the first witness to the Resurrection—what's more important than that, in Christianity? She was apostle to the apostles, told by Christ to go tell them he had risen."

—Susan Haskins, author of *Mary Magdalen: Myth and Metaphor*

"There was no such person in the history of the world as Jesus Christ. There was no historical, living, breathing, sentient human being by that name. Ever. [The Bible] is a fictional, non-historical narrative. The myth is good for business."

—Jon Murray, President of American Atheists

"Muslims see him as the greatest prophet before the prophet of Islam. He is the prophet of inward spiritual life.

Islam does not accept that he was crucified, died, then was resurrected. Islam believes he was taken to heaven without dying, without suffering the pain of death."

—Seyyed Hossein Nasr, Professor of Islamic studies at George Washington University

The above quotations are excerpted from Life magazine, December 1994.

Permission to photocopy this handout from Group's Core Belief Bible Study Series granted for local church use.
Copyright © Group Publishing, Inc., P.O. Box 481, Loveland, CO 80539.

THE ISSUE: Gray Areas of Scripture

Out of the Gray

Helping Kids Apply the Bible to Their World

by Jane Vogel

THE POINT:
The Bible is relevant to your life.

■ If you ask teenagers what the Bible is about, you can probably guess some typical responses: ■ "It's about stuff that happened a long time ago." ■ "It's a book by old dead men." ■ "It's a bunch of confusing rules." ■ Some kids may understand that the Bible is God's Word for today, but they may not know how to apply it to their own lives and to the immediate circumstances they face. Where does the Bible talk about gangs? give guidelines for dating or choosing a college? address drugs, smoking, or any of the myriad of pressures a teenager faces at school? ■ Kids need to know that God's Word doesn't leave them to guess on their own. It offers guidelines and principles that can be applied to every situation they face. When students learn to search for these principles and apply them to their lives, they'll begin to see that the Bible is a powerful and relevant guide for life.

The Study
AT A GLANCE

SECTION	MINUTES	WHAT STUDENTS WILL DO	SUPPLIES
Introductory Investigation	10 to 15	GRAY AREAS—Create a list of issues that are clearly right, clearly wrong, or in the "gray area."	Paper, pencils, newsprint, a marker, tape
Biblical Debate	25 to 35	A MATTER OF CONSCIENCE—Create skits and debates about applying the Bible to real-life "gray areas."	Bibles, pencils, "Resolved..." handout (p. 42)
Affirmation and Application	10 to 15	ACTING ON PRINCIPLE—Brainstorm biblical principles that apply to specific personal concerns.	Bibles, pencils, "Acting on Principle" handout (p. 43)

notes:

THE POINT OF *OUT OF THE GRAY:*

The Bible is relevant to your life.

THE BIBLE CONNECTION

1 CORINTHIANS 8:1-13 — Paul gives instructions about eating meat that is offered to idols.

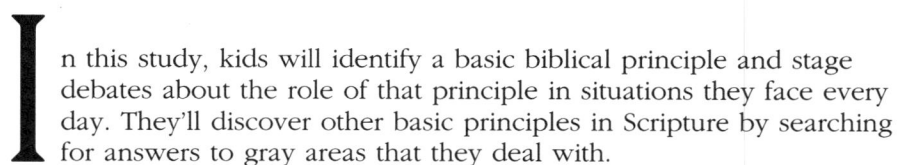

In this study, kids will identify a basic biblical principle and stage debates about the role of that principle in situations they face every day. They'll discover other basic principles in Scripture by searching for answers to gray areas that they deal with.

By applying biblical principles to the real-life issues they face, kids will discover immediate guidance for tough decisions and develop the skills needed to turn to the Bible for direction in those decisions.

Explore the verses in the Bible Connection, then study the information in the Depthfinder boxes throughout the study to gain a deeper understanding of how these Scriptures connect with your young people.

THE STUDY

INTRODUCTORY INVESTIGATION ▼

Gray Areas (10 to 15 minutes) Have kids form groups of three. Give each group a sheet of paper and a pencil. Ask each group to choose a Recorder and a Reporter. Have the Recorders draw vertical lines down their sheets of paper to create three columns of equal size. Have kids write "Definitely Wrong" at the top of the first column, "Gray Areas" at the top of the middle column, and "Definitely OK" at the top of the last column.

Say: **In the first column on your sheet of paper, have your Recorder list at least three actions you would all definitely agree are wrong. In last column, have your Recorder list at least three actions**

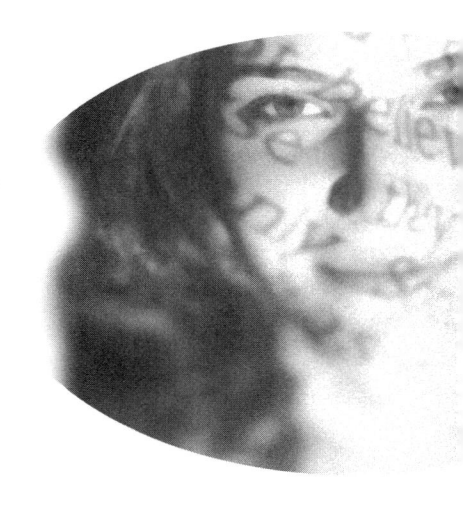

LEADER TIP for The Study

Whenever groups discuss a list of questions, write the questions on newsprint and tape the newsprint to the wall so groups can discuss the questions at their own pace.

> **LEADER TIP for The Study**
>
> Because this topic can be so powerful and relevant to kids' lives, your group members may be tempted to get caught up in issues and lose sight of the deeper biblical principle found in The Point. Help your kids grasp The Point by guiding them to focus on the biblical investigation and discussing how God's truth connects with reality in their lives.

DEPTHFINDER: SUPERPREDATORS

A Newsweek magazine article titled "'Superpredators' Arrive" (Peter Annin, Newsweek, January 22, 1996) states:

Criminal-justice experts have predicted the arrival of the superpredators—a generation of teens so numerous and savage that they'll take violence to a new level. "It's 'Lord of the Flies' on a massive scale," says Cook County State's Attorney Jack O'Malley. "We've become a nation being terrorized by our children."

In an article in the Wall Street Journal, Charles Colson comments on the findings of the Bipartisan Council on Crime in America. They warn that by the year 2000, children ages fourteen to seventeen will terrorize society like "teenage wolf packs." (Peter Boelens, "We Must Fill the Vacuum," The Luke Society News)

What causes the crime that fuels these dire predictions? John J. DiIulio Jr., a professor of politics and public affairs at Princeton, says these superpredators are deprived of "the benefit of parents, teachers, coaches and clergy to teach them right or wrong and show them unconditional love." (Richard Zoglin, "Now for the Bad News: A Teenage Time Bomb," Time, January 15, 1996)

As a youth leader, you're on the last line of defense in protecting our kids from the superpredator mentality. You have the unique opportunity to show unconditional love to this generation. You can teach them to search God's Word to discover the difference between right and wrong. You can help protect them from the devastation and desperation of becoming a superpredator.

that are definitely right. In the middle column, have your Recorder list at least three actions that you think fall into the gray area.

While the groups are working, use the marker and a sheet of newsprint to create a large version of the three-column work sheets that the kids made. Tape the large work sheet to a wall.

Call the kids back together. Ask the Reporters to read the actions their groups came up with. Have the Recorders write the actions in the appropriate columns on the newsprint work sheet that you taped to the wall.

Ask:
- **Do you think the Bible effectively addresses the issues that the youth of today face? Why or why not?**
- **How would you make the decision whether to participate in something listed in the gray area?**
- **How can the Bible help you know what to do about a situation that isn't directly discussed in Scripture?**
- **Do you think <u>the Bible is relevant to your life</u>? Why or why not?**

Say: **The Bible doesn't directly address many of the issues that we face. However, it does give principles and guidelines that we can apply to any situation. Let me show you what I mean.**

DEPTH FINDER: CAN SOMETHING BE RIGHT FOR ONE PERSON AND WRONG FOR ANOTHER?

In this age of situational ethics, it may be a little disconcerting to find that Paul suggests that what's right and wrong depends on...who you're with at the time!

Of course, some things are wrong no matter what: selfishness, envy, and the attitudes and actions that flow from them. But some actions really aren't morally wrong in themselves; it's their impact on others that makes them harmful.

In Paul's culture, the meat offered for sale in the marketplace had sometimes first been offered to an idol. After the ritual ceremony had been performed, the meat could be sold.

Early Christians needed to know if they were sinning by eating this meat. Were they in some way participating in the idol sacrifice if they bought the meat? What if they ate it without knowing where it came from? Where they still culpable?

Paul's direction to the people of Corinth was simple: Idols aren't real. They can't do anything to you, and neither can the meat sacrificed to them. There's no reason to worry about eating the meat.

But if you still feel guilty, don't eat it. You can't be healthy spiritually if you think you're doing something wrong. And if someone around you thinks it's wrong, then you shouldn't do it either. Make certain your action doesn't offend that person or tempt him or her to act against his or her conscience.

The importance isn't in what you eat, but in whether you are trying to nurture your own spiritual growth and that of those around you.

> **LEADER TIP for A Matter of Conscience**
>
> If you don't have enough time to allow all the groups to stage their situations, you can either stage two or more simultaneously in different areas of your meeting place or choose just a few of the groups to present their situations.

BIBLICAL DEBATE ▼

A Matter of Conscience (25 to 35 minutes) Have students return to their threesomes. Ask the group members who didn't act as Recorders or Reporters in the first activity to read aloud 1 Corinthians 8:1-13. Have groups discuss these questions:

● **Why were the Christians in Corinth confused over the issue of eating meat that had been offered to idols?**

● **What principles did Paul give to help Christians decide how to act when they encountered the issue of eating meat that was offered to idols?**

● **Are these principles relevant to your life? If so, how? If not, why not?**

Have each threesome choose one of the gray areas that they listed on the sheet of newsprint in the "Gray Areas" activity. Encourage each group to take a different situation. Give each teenager a copy of the "Resolved..." handout (p. 42) and a pencil, and ask them to read the guidelines for their presentations. Answer any questions the students have. Then have the threesomes discuss their situations within their groups and prepare for their presentations.

Call the kids back together. Have the groups take turns presenting their situations according to the format in the handout. After each presentation, allow

> **LEADER TIP for A Matter of Conscience**
>
> To bring a creative edge to this activity, set props out in the middle of the room for kids to use as they prepare for their presentations. Let them know that they can use the props to help them act out their situations. Some prop ideas include: hats, coats, wigs, books, paper, a bowling ball, tools, blankets, a phone, and a clock.

> # DEPTH FINDER
> ## TRUTH OR CONSEQUENCES
>
> Teenagers don't always recognize the consequences of their actions. Disobedience, even to God's commands, may seem immaterial. They may argue that, since God will forgive them, it's not really a big deal if they make the wrong choice—especially if they aren't hurting anyone else. But disobeying God's laws often hurts people—not necessarily as a punishment, but as a natural consequence. For example:
> - Sex outside of marriage can result in a damaged reputation, loss of self-respect, sexually transmitted disease, and unwanted pregnancy.
> - Cheating can lead to a failing grade and failure to learn to make it on your own.
> - Drunkenness can lead to addiction, health problems, failed relationships, lost jobs, and fatal automobile accidents.
> - Stealing can lead to a criminal record and broken trust. It can blunt the thief's conscience, lead to other crimes, or saddle him or her with crippling guilt.
> - Gossip ruins friendships, gives the gossip the reputation of being two-faced, and leaves him or her wondering what people are saying when he or she isn't nearby.

time for the other students to discuss and comment on the suggested application of 1 Corinthians 8:1-13. Prompt discussion with questions such as:

- **Do you think what the Bible says is relevant in this situation? Why or why not?**
- **Is there a time when this action isn't OK? Explain.**
- **Is there a time when this action is OK? Explain.**
- **What's the best way to handle this situation? Why do you think so?**

After all the groups have presented their situations, ask:

- **When would it be hard for you to give up your right to do something that isn't wrong?**
- **Have you ever done something that you believed was OK to do, but someone else thought it was wrong? If so, what happened? How did you feel?**
- **Have you ever seen another Christian do something you thought was wrong? How did it affect you?**
- **Do you think that <u>the Bible is relevant to your life</u>? Why or why not?**

Say: **1 Corinthians 8:1-13 seems to be pretty irrelevant to today's culture. You probably don't spend much time worrying about whether the food you eat has been offered to idols. But if you look beyond the circumstances of this passage to the principles, you'll find that God has given an excellent example to help you determine how to use the freedom he has given you. This is an issue that every Christian must deal with. As you learn to look beyond the surface and search for the principles in God's Word, you'll find that <u>the Bible is relevant to your life.</u>**

Out of the Gray   40

AFFIRMATION AND APPLICATION ▼

Acting on Principle
(10 to 15 minutes)

Have kids return to their trios. Then say: **Let each person in your group share a gray-area issue that he or she struggles with. Then pray for the person on your right. Ask God to help that person find and apply God's principles to his or her gray area.**

Distribute the "Acting on Principle" handout (p. 43) and pencils. Say: **Use this handout to brainstorm biblical principles that address a gray area you sometimes struggle with and to find ways that the Bible is relevant to your life. Discuss how you can apply those principles to your situation. Be sure to circle or jot down the principles that apply to your own gray area.**

When kids finish, ask:

● **Were you able to find biblical principles that addressed your gray area?**

● **What's the best way to deal with your gray area?**

● **Are there any areas of life that the Bible doesn't help us deal with? Explain.**

Say: **It isn't always easy to act on the principles you uncover. But you've probably already had some practice, maybe without even realizing it. Look at the principles the other people in your trio circled or jotted down on their sheets. Take a minute to recall ways you've seen them act on those principles in the past. Then take turns telling about the principles you've already seen at work in each other's lives.**

LEADER TIP for Acting on Principle

To supplement the "Acting on Principle" handout (p. 43), you can provide other resources to help your students find appropriate Scripture passages for their gray areas:

● Concordances can be helpful if a student has a particular passage in mind but doesn't know where to find it. They're of limited use in looking up certain topics because many of the gray areas your students wonder about will likely relate to contemporary issues that are not specifically mentioned (for example: drug use, choice of music or movies, and dating questions).

● Many study Bibles have lists that point readers to specific passages. *The Youth Bible*, for example, has a "Topical Devotion Guide" listing a variety of topics such as anger, depression, school, and sexuality. *The Student Bible* (NIV) contains a "Subject Guide" that lists passages dealing with subjects of interest including abortion, homosexuality, popularity, and suicide.

Resolved...

As a threesome, choose one of the gray-area situations listed earlier, and discuss it together. Each of you should choose one of the three roles (Person, Persuader, and Dissuader) explained below. Then plan together how you'll present your situation for the "Set the Stage" part of this activity. After you have planned your skit, take a few minutes alone to prepare your arguments and responses.

THE ROLES

The Persuader
- During "Set the Stage," act out whatever role is needed to clearly demonstrate the situation that the Person is facing.
- During "Convince the Person," act as the conscience of the Person. Your goal is to convince the Person to choose to participate in the gray area. Use the Bible, logic, and emotions in any way you can to convince the person to participate. After the Person has finished asking questions, debate the holes or weaknesses you saw in the Dissuader's argument.

The Person
- During "Set the Stage," act as the one who must decide whether or not to participate in the gray area. Play the part of someone who isn't certain what to do.
- During "Convince the Person," listen to what others say, then ask questions of the Dissuader and the Persuader. Try to address the holes you see in their arguments.
- During "The Decision," make a choice and explain why you chose it. Use 1 Corinthians 8:1-13 as your guide, and explain to the group how the passage applies to your gray area.

The Dissuader
- During "Set the Stage," act out whatever role is needed to clearly demonstrate the situation that the Person is facing.
- During "Convince the Person," act as the conscience of the Person. Your goal is to convince the Person to refrain from participating in the gray area. Use the Bible, logic, and emotions in any way you can to convince the person not to participate. After the Person has finished asking questions, debate the holes or weaknesses you saw in the Persuader's argument.

Follow this format to present your situation:

THE FORMAT

1. Set the Stage
- All three of you are the actors in this part. You need to show everyone what decision the Person must make by acting out an event that leads the Person to decide if he or she will participate in your gray area.
- Set the stage for the Person's choice, and stop the skit right before the Person must make the choice.
- Try to present circumstances in which the choice is not obvious. For example, if your gray area is drinking alcohol, don't present a situation in which the Person must decide whether he or she should slam beers until he or she passes out. Instead, present a situation in which the Person must decide whether he or she will accept a drink that was offered by his or her parents.

2. Convince the Person
- After you have stopped the skit, wait for a few seconds. The Persuader and Dissuader should stand on opposite sides of the Person.
- The Persuader has one minute to convince the Person to participate in the gray area. The Person and the Dissuader may not respond or talk while the Persuader is speaking.
- The Dissuader has one minute to convince the Person not to participate in the gray area. The Person and the Persuader may not respond while the Dissuader is speaking.
- After the Persuader and the Dissuader have presented their arguments, the Person may question both of them. Then the Persuader and the Dissuader may refute each other's arguments through debate.

3. The Decision
- After the Persuader and the Dissuader have debated, the Person must make a choice to participate in or refrain from participating in the gray area. The Person must explain his or her choice and why he or she made the choice.

Permission to photocopy this handout from Group's Core Belief Bible Study Series granted for local church use.
Copyright © Group Publishing, Inc., P.O. Box 481, Loveland, CO 80539.

Acting on Principle

The Bible doesn't always directly address the situations we find ourselves in. But the principles in the Bible are always relevant to our lives.

Here are some general biblical principles. Read them, look up the passages that seem most appropriate, and discuss in your trio how one or more of these principles apply to the specific situation you are facing. Circle or jot down the principles that seem most relevant to your own personal gray-area situation.

Principle	Where to Find It
If it brings blessings, do it.	Deuteronomy 30:19-20
If it points others to God, do it.	Matthew 5:13-16
If it hurts someone else in any way, don't do it.	Matthew 7:12
If it's illegal, don't do it.	Romans 13:1-5
If it's bad for you physically, don't do it.	1 Corinthians 6:12-20
If it goes against your parent's wishes, don't do it.	Ephesians 6:1-3
If it puts others first, do it.	Philippians 2:1-11
If it honors Jesus Christ, do it.	Colossians 3:17

Permission to photocopy this handout from Group's Core Belief Bible Study Series granted for local church use. Copyright © Group Publishing, Inc., P.O. Box 481, Loveland, CO 80539.

THE ISSUE: Isolation

All by Myself

Helping Young People Break Down the Walls of Their Isolation

by Lisa Baba Lauffer

THE POINT: The Bible is God's Word to us.

■ The television blares and flashes pictures of friends sharing secrets. The radio squawks as the talk show host refutes the arguments of a caller. On the computer, words come scrolling in from across the continent or maybe across the world, and at the same time, the young person talks on the phone with a classmate. ■ Despite all these simultaneous visual and auditory inputs, that young person is all alone... ■ Our society continues to make it easier and easier for people to get around without hearing, seeing, or touching other people. And that ease of virtual societal navigation makes it difficult for teenagers to connect. ■ Yet they're never truly alone. They can find a personal connection in something that began thousands of years ago and has transcended all the methods of connecting that this world has devised. It has outlived the Pony Express, carrier pigeons, and the telegraph, and it will outlast cellular phones, pagers, and the World Wide Web. ■ What is this incredible, transcendent method of connection? It's God's Word, written as a love letter to each of us. This study will show your students how the Bible can help them overcome their isolation.

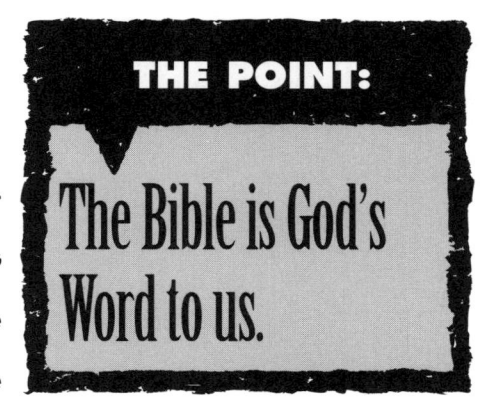

The Study
AT A GLANCE

SECTION	MINUTES	WHAT STUDENTS WILL DO	SUPPLIES
Isolation Experience	15 to 20	ISOLATION WARD—Construct walls that separate them from each other, them answer questions about their experience with isolation.	Cardboard, duct tape, markers, "You're on Your Own" handout (p. 51)
Interactive Discussion	10 to 15	BREAKING THROUGH—Cut through the walls between them and discuss questions from the "You're on Your Own" and "You're in This Together" handouts.	Scissors, "You're on Your Own" handout (p. 51), "You're in This Together" handout (p. 52)
Interactive Bible Exploration	15 to 20	GOD'S TOUCH—Explore Bible passages that explain how God can speak to them through his Word, then read passages that address issues contributing to their sense of isolation.	Bibles, "You're Never Alone" handout (p. 53), scissors, markers
Closing	5 to 10	THE WALLS COME TUMBLING DOWN—Tear down their cardboard walls as they list Bible truths that can minister to someone who feels isolated.	

notes:

THE POINT OF *ALL BY MYSELF:*

The Bible is God's Word to us.

THE BIBLE CONNECTION	
1 THESSALONIANS 1:4-6	Paul reveals the Source of the Good News.
2 PETER 1:19-21	Peter explains how God used the prophets to create Scripture.

In this study, kids will create an "isolation ward" and spend some time alone evaluating their level of isolation in real life. Then they'll create passageways to others and explore Scriptures that describe how God speaks to them through the Bible.

Explore the verses in The Bible Connection, then examine the information in the Depthfinder boxes throughout the study to gain a deeper understanding of how these Scriptures connect with your young people.

THE STUDY

ISOLATION EXPERIENCE ▼

Isolation Ward (15 to 20 minutes) Before the study, set out the cardboard and the duct tape. When everyone has arrived, say: **We're going to create an "isolation ward" in this room. Each of you must create your own isolation cell using the supplies I've provided. As you do this, make sure you share a wall with at least one other person in the room, if not more. But you must cordon yourself off from everyone else. No speaking is allowed during this activity. You have ten minutes to build your cell.**

As students create their isolation cells, make sure that each student shares a wall with at least one other person. If someone hasn't done this,

> **LEADER TIP for Isolation Ward**
>
> If you can't gather enough duct tape and cardboard for kids to create walls between one another, students can use masking tape to hang old sheets of newsprint or newspaper from the ceiling of your meeting room. Make sure you use materials that kids can write on.

All by Myself 47

LEADER TIP for Isolation Ward

For safety purposes, encourage kids to create their isolation cells with at least one wall they can open and shut.

LEADER TIP for The Study

Because this topic can be so powerful and relevant to kids' lives, your group members may be tempted to get caught up in issues and lose sight of the deeper biblical principle found in The Point. Help your kids grasp The Point by guiding them to focus on the biblical investigation and discussing how God's truth connects with reality in their lives.

silently direct that person to a place where he or she can build a wall between him- or herself and another person. Also, as students build, mentally note to yourself pairs who share walls with each other. You'll need to direct students to pair up later in the study, and pairs will need to be formed according to those who share walls.

When everyone has finished creating his or her cell, walk around the room and drop a "You're on Your Own" handout (p. 51) and a marker into each cell. Allow kids five to ten minutes to complete the handout by writing their answers on the walls of their cells.

As kids write, peek into their cells from time to time to gauge their progress. When everyone has finished writing answers to the questions, move on to the Interactive Discussion section.

DEPTH FINDER — UNDERSTANDING ISOLATION IN OUR SOCIETY

Many people look at today's young people and deride them for isolating themselves from the world by plopping themselves in front of their televisions and computers to the exclusion of real-life relationships. But according to senior news editor Tom R. Halfhill in his Byte article "The Introversion of America," this is no new phenomenon. Halfhill says

> Over the years, that connection to the outside world has gradually been replaced with electronics that span great distances. First telephones, then radio, then TV, and now computers have changed the way we socialize, maintain relationships, and relate to our neighbors. Most recently, millions of people have started communicating with each other via computers and modems plugged into online networks—and soon, via the data superhighway.

We can't fault our young people for isolating themselves through technology; this has been a cultural trend for years, one that kids fit right into.

Though we can't fault them for it, we can encourage them to buck the trend to some extent. Technology is good, but when we overdose on it, it hinders our ability to relate to others and contributes to our sense of isolation. Halfhill says, "Nowadays, modern transportation and communication free us to associate with those who share our views and interests, and that's good. But they also threaten to isolate us from our immediate communities, and that's bad."

As you teach this study, encourage kids to determine their level of isolation. If they feel isolated from others, ask them what factors contribute to their isolation. If they're astute about their habits, many kids will identify overinvolvement with television and computers as a contributor. If so, invite your young people to reduce the amount of time they spend with these things. Perhaps you could institute a group challenge in which you and your students agree to, for one week, limit hours spent watching TV, playing video games, and chatting online. Have kids pair up as accountability partners. You can even encourage kids to spend their extra time with their accountability partners as a proactive way of building relationships that can diminish their isolation. After a week, have kids share their experiences with the group, including any new insights gained from the experiment. Encourage your kids to pursue real-life relationships, being intimate with people they can trust so they don't experience so much isolation in our technology-based society.

All by Myself

DEPTH FINDER: A BENEFIT OF RELATING

According to a variety of studies, conquering isolation can bolster one's health. "If you want to cheat death, form friendships, studies suggest. People—including the chronically ill—who have good social networks tend to outlive others who lack that support."

("Death comes knocking when you're alone," Science News, September 3, 1994)

INTERACTIVE DISCUSSION ▼

Breaking Through (10 to 15 minutes) Hand scissors to one person from each pair you mentally noted during the previous activity. Whisper to that person to cut a door in the wall he or she shares with his or her partner and go through the door. As you direct students to do this, make sure no one is left out. If necessary, have a pair cut through a wall to a third person to form a trio. Then say: **Now that you've made a connection with someone near you, show and explain to your partner the answers you've written on the walls of your isolation cell.** Make sure that both partners share.

When partners have finished showing each other around their cells, have each pair sit in one partner's cell. Hand each pair a "You're in This

DEPTH FINDER: UNDERSTANDING THE BIBLE

So often when we feel alone and isolated, we wish God would come down and touch us. We want him to intervene in our lives, to give us a word to hold onto and tangible knowledge of his love. He has done that very thing by giving us the Bible. In 1 Thessalonians 1:4-6, Paul explains that God wrote his Word to us because he loves us, reaching down to us through the Holy Spirit that we might experience his power. *The Disciple's Study Bible* further expounds on this passage: "Without God's love there would be no gospel. The whole Bible is, in a sense, the unfolding story of God's love."

In 2 Peter 1:19-21, Peter confirms Paul's claim, describing how, speaking through the Holy Spirit, God wrote the Scriptures through the prophets. *The Disciple's Study Bible* also interprets this passage, saying "Sacred writings have God as their source and are God-breathed (inspired by the presence of the Holy Spirit). Scripture is the truth of God put to writing in exactly the way God wanted it." God deliberately created the Bible as he did so that we might know and love him and discover how we can connect with him for eternity—through his Son Jesus Christ.

If we ever doubt the Bible's origins or that God could have possibly created such a tremendous work for us, we can bank on the truths of these and other Bible passages that explain the origins and purposes of Scripture. We may confidently believe in and live by the Bible as God's Word.

LEADER TIP for Breaking Through

Because kids will be scattered throughout the room in separate cells, large group discussion will be challenging. To engage kids when you talk with the whole group, either stand on a small stepladder so you can gain eye contact with kids in their cells, or designate a separate area of the room as a place to gather for large group discussion.

LEADER TIP for Breaking Through

Be certain to tell kids to avoid poking the person next to them as they cut the doors in the walls.

Together" handout (p. 52), and have partners go through it together.

When pairs have finished going through their handouts, say: **Most of us experience isolation at one time or another; many of us experience it a lot. But even when we feel most alone, we always have Someone who wants to reach out to us—God. He does this in so many ways, and one tangible way he reaches out to us is through the Bible, his Word to us.**

INTERACTIVE BIBLE EXPLORATION ▼

God's Touch (15 to 20 minutes)
Hand each student a "You're Never Alone" handout (p. 53) and a marker, and make sure pairs have Bibles and scissors. Have pairs go through the handout together.

When pairs have finished their discussions, invite students to share their insights from the Bible exploration with the whole class. Then say: **Because the Bible is God's Word to us, we can go to it whenever we have a struggle that isolates us from others. No matter how alone we feel, God will always reach out to us through his Word. To remind yourself of this, take a piece of your isolation cell home with you. Whenever you feel isolated, allow this piece of wall to encourage and remind you that God will touch you through his Word.**

CLOSING ▼

The Walls Come Tumbling Down (5 to 10 minutes)
Say: **Because God wants to and can reach us through our isolation, let's break down the walls we've built today.** Have students brainstorm things God says in his Word that can minister to someone who feels isolated; for example, God loves us, God is always with us, or God cares when we hurt. For each statement mentioned, have students tear down one of the walls that were built at the beginning of the study.

Close the meeting by thanking God for the power of his Word to break through our isolation.

LEADER TIP for Breaking Through

Students may have difficulty remaining silent during this activity. Use their restlessness as an opportunity to teach them about our need for one another and the discomfort isolation causes.

LEADER TIP for God's Touch

If possible, provide additional Bible resources such as concordances and topical Bibles for kids to use as they look for verses that address their issues. During the activity, circulate among the pairs to assist kids in finding appropriate Bible passages.

All by Myself   50

You're on your Own

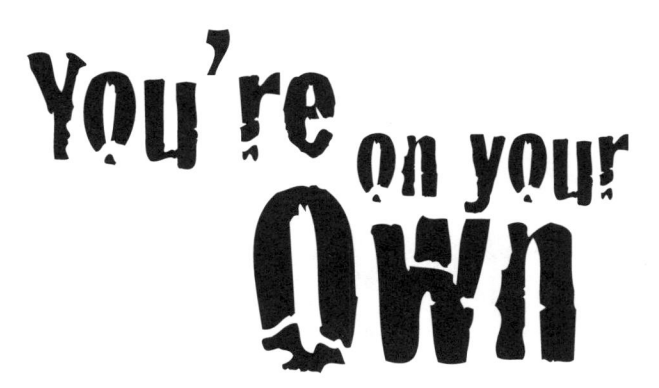

Now that you've isolated yourself from the others in this room, please take some time to answer the questions below. Write your answers on the walls of your cell. Remain silent as you do this activity.

- **What's your reaction to being isolated from everyone else in the room?**

- **What were you thinking and feeling as you built walls between yourself and the others in this room? as you saw others build walls between themselves and you?**

- **How is the way you built physical walls between yourself and others in this room like the ways people build emotional walls between themselves and others? How is it different?**

- **On a scale from 1 to 143, with 1 being "I never feel isolated" and 143 being "I always feel isolated," what would you rate your level of isolation in real life? Why?**

- **If you rated your isolation level greater than 1, what situations most often make you feel isolated? Why?**

- **When you feel isolated, what do you most need from others? from yourself?**

Now that you've finished answering the questions, please sit quietly in your cell until you receive further instructions. If you wish, write any other thoughts or feelings you have about the topic of isolation. If you're artistically inclined, you could draw a picture of what you think isolation looks like.

Permission to photocopy this handout from Group's Core Belief Bible Study Series granted for local church use. Copyright © Group Publishing, Inc., P.O. Box 481, Loveland, CO 80539.

You're in this Together

Now that you've made a connection with someone else in the room and shared your answers to the previous questions, discuss these questions:

- **How do you feel now that you've made a connection with someone else?**

- **What were you thinking and feeling as you cut through the wall and entered someone else's cell or as your partner cut a door to you and came into your cell? as you shared your answers to the questions from the first handout?**

- **How was the way you reacted like the way you react when someone reaches out to you when you feel isolated? like the way you react when you reach out to someone else who feels isolated? How is it different?**

- **Have you ever experienced God reaching out to you when you've felt isolated? If so, how? What was your response?**

- **Do you know that the Bible is God's Word to you? What's your reaction to that truth?**

Before we go to the next part of the study, pray for each other. Pray that God would help each of you to endure your isolation and to connect with others. Then pray that, through the rest of this study, God will show you how he reaches out to you every day.

Permission to photocopy this handout from Group's Core Belief Bible Study Series granted for local church use.
Copyright © Group Publishing, Inc., P.O. Box 481, Loveland, CO 80539.

You're never Alone

Read 1 Thessalonians 1:4-6 and 2 Peter 1:19-21, and discuss these questions with your partner:
- What do these passages say about how the Bible is God's Word to us?
- How do you feel, knowing that God speaks to you through his Word?
- How can the Bible help you when you feel isolated?

Think of an issue you're dealing with that makes you feel isolated. Maybe you feel rejected by a friend. Perhaps you feel like you're facing your future alone. When you've thought of your issue, cut out a blank piece of wall from your isolation cell, and write your issue on it. Tell your partner what you've written.

Then, as a pair, look for what the Bible says about both of your issues. Remember, the Bible is God's Word to you, so God will speak to you through it, even about the issues that make you feel the most isolated. Listed below are just a few struggles that might make you feel isolated and Bible passages that address those issues. Find the area that most closely resembles the subject about which you need to hear from God. Then look up and read aloud the passage(s) listed next to that issue.

betrayal—Psalm 55:12-14, 16-23

conflicts with friends—Ephesians 4:2-6, 31-32

doubts about God—John 20:19-31

facing your own wrongdoing—1 John 1:8-9; 1 Timothy 1:12-17

family struggles—Matthew 5:23-24; Mark 3:31-35; Ephesians 6:1-4

feeling afraid—Psalm 27:1-3; Matthew 14:22-33

feeling depressed—Psalm 40:1-5; Isaiah 35

feeling discouraged—1 John 5:13-15

feeling misunderstood—Hebrews 4:14-16

the future—Jeremiah 29:11-13; Matthew 6:34

inadequacy—1 Samuel 16:1-13; Psalm 8

isolating illness—2 Corinthians 12:7-10

isolation and loneliness—Matthew 28:20b; John 14:1-3, 15-21

not achieving popularity—1 Corinthians 3:4-9

rejection—Psalm 69:8-16, 33; Romans 15:4-7

resisting peer pressure—Psalm 1:1-3

romantic relationships—1 Corinthians 13; 1 Peter 1:22

saying goodbye to someone you love—2 Kings 2:1-15

school struggles—Proverbs 2:1-10; 9:8-12

troubles—Romans 5:3-5; James 1:2-4

On your piece of wall, write what you think God, through his Word, is saying to you about your issue. Share what you've written with your partner, then discuss these questions:
- What's your reaction to reading what God says about your issue?
- How do you feel, knowing that God has put a special word in the Bible to you about your issue?
- How does this experience affect what you think about the Bible as God's Word to you?
- How does this experience affect what you'll do the next time you feel isolated from everybody?

Before we conclude this study, tell your partner one reason you enjoyed exploring the subject of isolation with him or her. For example, you might tell your partner that he or she was fun to be with or that you learned a lot from his or her insights.

Permission to photocopy this handout from Group's Core Belief Bible Study Series granted for local church use.
Copyright © Group Publishing, Inc., P.O. Box 481, Loveland, CO 80539.

why Active and Interactive Learning works with teenagers

Let's Start With the Big Picture

Think back to a major life lesson you've learned.
Got it? Now answer these questions:
- Did you learn your lesson from something you read?
- Did you learn it from something you heard?
- Did you learn it from something you experienced?

If you're like 99 percent of your peers, you answered "yes" only to the third question—you learned your life lesson from something you experienced.

This simple test illustrates the most convincing reason for using active and interactive learning with young people: People learn best through experience. Or to put it even more simply, people learn by doing.

Learning by doing is what active learning is all about. No more sitting quietly in chairs and listening to a speaker expound theories about God—that's passive learning. Active learning gets kids out of their chairs and into the experience of life. With active learning, kids get to *do* what they're studying. They *feel* the effects of the principles you teach. They *learn* by experiencing truth firsthand.

Active learning works because it recognizes three basic learning needs and uses them in concert to enable young people to make discoveries on their own and to find practical life applications for the truths they believe.

So what are these three basic learning needs?
1. Teenagers need action.
2. Teenagers need to think.
3. Teenagers need to talk.

Read on to find out exactly how these needs will be met by using the active and interactive learning techniques in Group's Core Belief Bible Study Series in your youth group.

1. Teenagers Need Action

Aircraft pilots know well the difference between passive and active learning. Their passive learning comes through listening to flight instructors and reading flight-instruction books. Their active learning comes

Helpful Stuff 55

through actually flying an airplane or flight simulator. Books and lectures may be helpful, but pilots really learn to fly by manipulating a plane's controls themselves.

We can help young people learn in a similar way. Though we may engage students passively in some reading and listening to teachers, their understanding and application of God's Word will really take off through simulated and real-life experiences.

Forms of active learning include simulation games; role-plays; service projects; experiments; research projects; group pantomimes; mock trials; construction projects; purposeful games; field trips; and, of course, the most powerful form of active learning—real-life experiences.

We can more fully explain active learning by exploring four of its characteristics:

- **Active learning is an adventure.** Passive learning is almost always predictable. Students sit passively while the teacher or speaker follows a planned outline or script.

In active learning, kids may learn lessons the teacher never envisioned. Because the leader trusts students to help create the learning experience, learners may venture into unforeseen discoveries. And often the teacher learns as much as the students.

- **Active learning is fun and captivating.** What are we communicating when we say, "OK, the fun's over—time to talk about God"? What's the hidden message? That joy is separate from God? And that learning is separate from joy?

What a shame.

Active learning is not joyless. One seventh-grader we interviewed clearly remembered her best Sunday school lesson: "Jesus was the light, and we went into a dark room and shut off the lights. We had a candle, and we learned that Jesus is the light and the dark can't shut off the light." That's active learning. Deena enjoyed the lesson. She had fun. And she learned.

Active learning intrigues people. Whether they find a foot-washing experience captivating or maybe a bit uncomfortable, they learn. And they learn on a level deeper than any work sheet or teacher's lecture could ever reach.

- **Active learning involves everyone.** Here the difference between passive and active learning becomes abundantly clear. It's like the difference between watching a football game on television and actually playing in the game.

The "trust walk" provides a good example of involving everyone in active learning. Half of the group members put on blindfolds; the other half serve as guides. The "blind" people trust the guides to lead them through the building or outdoors. The guides prevent the blind people from falling down stairs or tripping over rocks. Everyone needs to participate to learn the inherent lessons of trust, faith, doubt, fear, confidence, and servanthood. Passive spectators of this experience would learn little, but participants learn a great deal.

- **Active learning is focused through debriefing.** Activity simply for activity's sake doesn't usually result in good learning. Debriefing—evaluating an experience by discussing it in pairs or small groups—helps focus the experience and draw out its meaning. Debriefing helps

Helpful Stuff　56

sort and order the information students gather during the experience. It helps learners relate the recently experienced activity to their lives.

The process of debriefing is best started immediately after an experience. We use a three-step process in debriefing: reflection, interpretation, and application.

Reflection—This first step asks the students, "How did you feel?" Active-learning experiences typically evoke an emotional reaction, so it's appropriate to begin debriefing at that level.

Some people ask, "What do feelings have to do with education?" Feelings have everything to do with education. Think back again to that time in your life when you learned a big lesson. In all likelihood, strong feelings accompanied that lesson. Our emotions tend to cement things into our memories.

When you're debriefing, use open-ended questions to probe feelings. Avoid questions that can be answered with a "yes" or "no." Let your learners know that there are no wrong answers to these "feeling" questions. Everyone's feelings are valid.

Interpretation—The next step in the debriefing process asks, "What does this mean to you? How is this experience like or unlike some other aspect of your life?" Now you're asking people to identify a message or principle from the experience.

You want your learners to discover the message for themselves. So instead of telling students your answers, take the time to ask questions that encourage self-discovery. Use Scripture and discussion in pairs or small groups to explore how the actions and effects of the activity might translate to their lives.

Alert! Some of your people may interpret wonderful messages that you never intended. That's not failure! That's the Holy Spirit at work. God allows us to catch different glimpses of his kingdom even when we all look through the same glass.

Application—The final debriefing step asks, "What will you do about it?" This step moves learning into action. Your young people have shared a common experience. They've discovered a principle. Now they must create something new with what they've just experienced and interpreted. They must integrate the message into their lives.

The application stage of debriefing calls for a decision. Ask your students how they'll change, how they'll grow, what they'll do as a result of your time together.

2. Teenagers Need to Think

Today's students have been trained not to think. They aren't dumber than previous generations. We've simply conditioned them not to use their heads.

You see, we've trained our kids to respond with the simplistic answers they think the teacher wants to hear. Fill-in-the-blank student workbooks and teachers who ask dead-end questions such as "What's the capital of Delaware?" have produced kids and adults who have learned not to think.

And it doesn't just happen in junior high or high school. Our children are schooled very early not to think. Teachers attempt to help kids read with nonsensical fill-in-the-blank drills, word scrambles, and missing-letter puzzles.

Helping teenagers think requires a paradigm shift in how we teach. We need to plan for and set aside time for higher-order thinking and be willing to reduce our time spent on lower-order parroting. Group's Core Belief Bible Study Series is designed to help you do just that.

Thinking classrooms look quite different from traditional classrooms. In most church environments, the teacher does most of the talking and hopes that knowledge will transmit from his or her brain to the students'. In thinking settings, the teacher coaches students to ponder, wonder, imagine, and problem-solve.

3. Teenagers Need to Talk

Everyone knows that the person who learns the most in any class is the teacher. Explaining a concept to someone else is usually more helpful to the explainer than to the listener. So why not let the students do more teaching? That's one of the chief benefits of letting kids do the talking. This process is called interactive learning.

What is interactive learning? Interactive learning occurs when students discuss and work cooperatively in pairs or small groups.

Interactive learning encourages learners to work together. It honors the fact that students can learn from one another, not just from the teacher. Students work together in pairs or small groups to accomplish shared goals. They build together, discuss together, and present together. They teach each other and learn from one another. Success as a group is celebrated. Positive interdependence promotes individual and group learning.

Interactive learning not only helps people learn but also helps learners feel better about themselves and get along better with others. It accomplishes these things more effectively than the independent or competitive methods.

Here's a selection of interactive learning techniques that are used in Group's Core Belief Bible Study Series. With any of these models, leaders may assign students to specific partners or small groups. This will maximize cooperation and learning by preventing all the "rowdies" from linking up. And it will allow for new friendships to form outside of established cliques.

Following any period of partner or small-group work, the leader may reconvene the entire class for large-group processing. During this time the teacher may ask for reports or discoveries from individuals or teams. This technique builds in accountability for the teacherless pairs and small groups.

Pair-Share—With this technique each student turns to a partner and responds to a question or problem from the teacher or leader. Every learner responds. There are no passive observers. The teacher may then ask people to share their partners' responses.

Study Partners—Most curricula and most teachers call for Scripture passages to be read to the whole class by one person. One reads; the others doze.

Why not relinquish some teacher control and let partners read and react with each other? They'll all be involved—and will learn more.

Learning Groups—Students work together in small groups to create a model, design artwork, or study a passage or story; then they discuss what they learned through the experience. Each person in the learning group may be assigned a specific role. Here are some examples:

Reader

Recorder (makes notes of key thoughts expressed during the reading or discussion)

Checker (makes sure everyone understands and agrees with answers arrived at by the group)

Encourager (urges silent members to share their thoughts)

When everyone has a specific responsibility, knows what it is, and contributes to a small group, much is accomplished and much is learned.

Summary Partners—One student reads a paragraph, then the partner summarizes the paragraph or interprets its meaning. Partners alternate roles with each paragraph.

The paraphrasing technique also works well in discussions. Anyone who wishes to share a thought must first paraphrase what the previous person said. This sharpens listening skills and demonstrates the power of feedback communication.

Jigsaw—Each person in a small group examines a different concept, Scripture, or part of an issue. Then each teaches the others in the group. Thus, all members teach, and all must learn the others' discoveries. This technique is called a jigsaw because individuals are responsible to their group for different pieces of the puzzle.

JIGSAW EXAMPLE

Here's an example of a jigsaw.

Assign four-person teams. Have teammates each number off from one to four. Have all the Ones go to one corner of the room, all the Twos to another corner, and so on.

Tell team members they're responsible for learning information in their numbered corners and then for teaching their team members when they return to their original teams.

Give the following assignments to various groups:

Ones: Read Psalm 22. Discuss and list the prophecies made about Jesus.

Twos: Read Isaiah 52:13–53:12. Discuss and list the prophecies made about Jesus.

Threes: Read Matthew 27:1-32. Discuss and list the things that happened to Jesus.

Fours: Read Matthew 27:33-66. Discuss and list the things that happened to Jesus.

After the corner groups meet and discuss, instruct all learners to return to their original teams and report what they've learned. Then have each team determine which prophecies about Jesus were fulfilled in the passages from Matthew.

Call on various individuals in each team to report one or two prophecies that were fulfilled.

You Can Do It Too!

All this information may sound revolutionary to you, but it's really not. God has been using active and interactive learning to teach his people for generations. Just look at Abraham and Isaac, Jacob and Esau, Moses and the Israelites, Ruth and Boaz. And then there's Jesus, who used active learning all the time!

Group's Core Belief Bible Study Series makes it easy for you to use active and interactive learning with your group. The active and interactive elements are automatically built in! Just follow the outlines, and watch as your kids grow through experience and positive interaction with others.

> **FOR DEEPER STUDY**
>
> For more information on incorporating active and interactive learning into your work with teenagers, check out these resources:
>
> ● *Why Nobody Learns Much of Anything at Church: And How to Fix It,* by Thom and Joani Schultz (Group Publishing) and
> ● *Do It! Active Learning in Youth Ministry,* by Thom and Joani Schultz (Group Publishing).

your evaluation of

core belief
Bible Study Series for senior high

why THE BIBLE matters

Group Publishing, Inc.
Attention: Core Belief Talk-back
P.O. Box 481
Loveland, CO 80539
Fax: (970) 669-1994

Please help us continue to provide innovative and useful resources for ministry. After you've led the studies in this volume, take a moment to fill out this evaluation; then mail or fax it to us at the address above. Thanks!

● ● ● ● ● ●

1. As a whole, this book has been (circle one)

not very helpful   very helpful
1   2   3   4   5   6   7   8   9   10

2. The best things about this book:

3. How this book could be improved:

4. What I will change because of this book:

5. Would you be interested in field-testing future Core Belief Bible Studies and giving us your feedback? If so, please complete the information below:

Name _____

Street address _____

City _____ State _____ Zip _____

Daytime telephone (___) _____ Date _____

THANKS!

Permission to photocopy this evaluation from Group's Core Belief Bible Study Series granted for local church use.
Copyright © Group Publishing, Inc., P.O. Box 481, Loveland, CO 80539.

Give Your Teenagers a Solid Faith Foundation That Lasts a Lifetime!

Here are the *essentials* of the Christian life—core values teenagers *must* believe to make good decisions now...and build an *unshakable* lifelong faith. Developed by youth workers like you...field-tested with *real* youth groups in *real* churches...here's the meat your kids *must* have to grow spiritually—presented in a fun, involving way!

Each 4-session, **Core Belief Bible Study Series** book lets you easily...

- Lead deep, compelling, *relevant* discussions your kids won't want to miss...
- Involve teenagers in exploring life-changing truths...
- Ground your teenagers in God's Word...and
- Help kids create healthy relationships with each other—and you!
- **Plus you'll make an *eternal difference* in the lives of your kids** as you give them a solid faith foundation that stands firm on God's Word—with Group's **Core Belief Bible Study Series!**

Core Belief Bible Study Series lessons are flexible...and simple, step-by-step directions make leading your group easy whether you're a veteran youth worker or a first-time volunteer! Pick and choose which core beliefs your teenagers most need to explore! Each 4-session book is all you need for any size group!

Here are the Core Belief Bible Study Series titles already available...

Senior High Studies

Why **Being a Christian** Matters	ISBN 0-7644-0883-6
Why **God** Matters	ISBN 0-7644-0874-7
Why **Jesus Christ** Matters	ISBN 0-7644-0875-5
Why **Suffering** Matters	ISBN 0-7644-0879-8
Why the **Bible** Matters	ISBN 0-7644-0882-8
Why the **Holy Spirit** Matters	ISBN 0-7644-0876-3

Junior High/Middle School Studies

The Truth About **Being a Christian**	ISBN 0-7644-0859-3
The Truth About **God**	ISBN 0-7644-0850-X
The Truth About **Jesus Christ**	ISBN 0-7644-0851-8
The Truth About **Suffering**	ISBN 0-7644-0855-0
The Truth About the **Bible**	ISBN 0-7644-0858-5
The Truth About the **Holy Spirit**	ISBN 0-7644-0852-6

Order today from your local Christian bookstore, or write: Group Publishing, P.O. Box 485, Loveland, CO 80539.

Practical Resources for Your Youth Ministry

Fun & Rowdy

Here are teenagers' 25 favorite fun and rowdy songs, each complete with quick, on-the-spot activities that involve kids directly in the music and message of each tune.

And whether you play guitar or piano—you're covered! You get both piano accompaniment and guitar chords.

Youth workers, Sunday school teachers, youth worship leaders, and youth choirs will all applaud these most-requested, raise-the-rafters, upbeat songs.

ISBN 1-55945-475-X

Group's Best Discussion Launchers for Youth Ministry

You want your kids to open up. To get past giving you the "right" answers to share what they're *really* thinking and feeling.

No problem. Here's the definitive collection of Group's best-ever discussion launchers!

You'll get **thought-provoking questions** kids can't *resist* answering... **compelling quotes** that *demand* a response... and **quick activities** that pull kids into an experience they can't *wait* to talk about.

Add zing to your youth meetings... revive meetings that are drifting off-track... and comfortably approach sensitive topics like AIDS, war, cults, gangs, suicide, dating, parents, self-image, and more.

ISBN 0-7644-2023-2

You-Choose-the-Ending Skits for Youth Ministry
Stephen Parolini

There's nothing quite as boring as "Sunday school skits" with endings you can see a mile away. Your kids hate them. You hate them. *So quit doing them!*

Instead, try these 19 hot-topic skits *guaranteed* to keep your kids on the edge of their seats—because each skit has **three possible endings!**

You can choose the ending... flip a coin... or let your teenagers vote. No matter which ending you pick, you'll get a great discussion going about a topic kids care about!

Skits require few actors... little or no rehearsal... and many skits get your audience involved, too, for maximum impact. Included: no-fail discussion questions!

ISBN 1-55945-627-2

Order today from your local Christian bookstore, or write: Group Publishing, P.O. Box 485, Loveland, CO 80539.

More Practical Resources for Your Youth Ministry

Last Impressions: Unforgettable Closings for Youth Meetings

Here's a collection of over 170 of Group's best-ever low-prep (or no-prep!) meeting closings...and each is tied to a thought-provoking Bible passage! You'll be ready with thoughtful...affirming...issue-oriented...high-energy...prayerful...and servanthood closings—on a moment's notice!

1-55945-629-9

Ready-to-Use Letters for Youth Ministry
Tom Tozer

These 110 already-written letters cover practically any situation that arises in youth ministry. And the included IBM-compatible computer disk makes adapting these letters quick and easy. You'll save hours of administrative time with this handy resource!

1-55945-692-2

Get Real: Making Core Christian Beliefs Relevant to Teenagers
Mike Nappa, Amy Nappa & Michael D. Warden

Here are the 24 Bible truths that Christian teenagers *must* know to survive in an unbelieving world. Included: proven strategies for effectively communicating these core Christian beliefs into the chaotic, fast-paced youth culture.

1-55945-708-2

Growing Close

These 150 practical, quick ideas help break the ice when teenagers don't know each other and break down cliques that often form in groups. A must-have resource for youth workers, coaches, camp directors, and Christian school teachers.

1-55945-709-0

Order today from your local Christian bookstore, or write: Group Publishing, P.O. Box 485, Loveland, CO 80539.